Original title:
Fern-tastic Verses

Copyright © 2025 Creative Arts Management OÜ
All rights reserved.

Author: Amelia Montgomery
ISBN HARDBACK: 978-1-80566-596-0
ISBN PAPERBACK: 978-1-80566-881-7

## Verdant Visions

In a garden full of green,
Lies a creature, unseen.
When asked about its fate,
It laughed, 'I'm just late!'

With each leaf that it sways,
It dances through the days.
A wiggle and a spin,
It says, 'Now let's begin!'

## Spheres of Softness

A cushion of leafy delight,
Where bugs race in the night.
They whisper to the moon,
'We'll sing a funny tune!'

Rolling round in a ball,
They giggle, nearly fall.
Among the leaves so lush,
They find joy in the hush.

## Fern Fronds and Forgotten Trails

Through hidden paths we roam,
With ferns that call us home.
A tickle on our toes,
As we dance with the rows.

Forgotten trails we trace,
With laughter in the space.
'Who needs a map?' we say,
When fun leads the way!

## Hidden Treasures of the Timberlands

In the woods, treasures hide,
Like secrets, side by side.
A squirrel shouts with glee,
'Just you wait, you'll see!'

Among the trunks they peek,
A stash of giggles, cheek!
'What's this? A nutty prank!'
The laughter floods the bank!

## Beneath the Leafy Canopy

In the forest, green confetti,
Squirrels dance, a little sweaty.
Mushrooms giggle, what a sight,
Leaves whisper secrets late at night.

Chirping crickets, offbeat tune,
Sunbeams filter, afternoon.
Beneath the leaves, the fun won't cease,
Nature's joke, a leafy fleece.

## **Dances of the Frond**

Fronds twirl like they own the place,
Grasshoppers join in with grace.
A lizard prances, tail on high,
While butterflies waltz, oh my, oh my!

Sunshine showers down like cake,
Every step, a little quake.
In this dance, the day feels right,
Nature giggles in pure delight.

## Secrets in the Shade

Under branches, secrets swirled,
A raccoon juggles things unfurled.
A turtle winks, a leaf on head,
While shadows play a game instead.

In the cool of leafy nooks,
Quiet laughter, playful hooks.
Nature whispers, woes and cheer,
In the dark, it's all sincere.

## Nature's Spiral Symphony

Spirals rise, a leafy maze,
Nature's whimsy in a daze.
Every twist, a giggling bloom,
Bringing sunshine to the gloom.

With each step, a rustle, a song,
Nature's party, come along!
Join the jest, with roots and fronds,
In this world where laughter bonds.

## **Cradled by the Canopy**

In the woods where ferns grow high,
I found a squirrel wearing a tie.
He danced around, quite full of glee,
As if he owned the whole darn tree.

A raccoon clapped and joined the scene,
With moves so slick, it felt quite mean.
They spun around in leafy glee,
Creating quite the ruckus, you see!

## The Timeless Dance of Green

The fronds do twist and sway with pride,
As ants host parties side by side.
They serve up crumbs, a tasty treat,
While grasshoppers tap their little feet.

A frog dressed sharp in a bowler hat,
Complains the weather's far too flat.
He jumps through puddles like a star,
Singing 'Kiss the Houseplants' from afar!

## A Glimpse into Greenery

Peeking through the leaves, oh my!
A snail wearing boots, that's no lie!
He slithered past with quite the flair,
While butterflies twirled through the air.

A ladybug laughed, a spot on her back,
Said, 'You'll never beat me, I'm on the right track!'
While worms cheered on with soil so fine,
In this leafy world, we all feel divine!

## Threads of Earthly Wonder

Underneath the canopy wide,
A gnome threw a fit, oh what a ride!
He lost his hat, but gained a song,
As insects joined in, all day long.

A hedgehog rolled by, in quite a haste,
Declared that thorns are a big disgrace!
Yet in this chaos, laughter found ground,
In this happy forest, joy abounds!

## Invitations from the Inwood

In the forest, trees do dance,
With squirrels prancing, taking a chance.
They send invites, all aglow,
To wiggle and giggle, oh what a show!

The mushrooms wear hats, a sight to see,
While rabbits sip tea, feeling quite free.
A party of critters, a jolly affair,
Don't mind the skunk, with his funky hair!

The wise old owl hoots a tune so bright,
As raccoons moonwalk under the moonlight.
Balloons made of leaves, hanging high,
"Join us!" they shout, "Don't be shy!"

So, take a stroll, don't miss out the fun,
In this woodland bash, where laughter's begun.
With foliage friends, you'll surely align,
Under a canopy, oh how divine!

## **The Green Canvases**

In gardens so lush, with colors so bold,
The plants all gather, stories unfold.
A painter's delight, nature's own brush,
With shades so vibrant, there's no need to rush!

The daisies gossip, the roses all jest,
While daisies challenge the bees to a quest.
They've painted the soil with whimsical scenes,
While beetles play tag in their shiny machines!

A peacock struts with feathers so grand,
Telling the sun to lend him a hand.
"Give me some sparkle, a bit of bling,
For every green canvas, I want to sing!"

With laughter erupting from every petal,
Nature's a clown, a joyous medal.
Join in the fun, where artistry thrives,
In these green canvases, imagination drives!

## Nature's Garden of Whispers

In whispers and giggles, the flowers conspire,
Their tales of the wind could spark a fire.
"Did you hear that?" a tulip does say,
"Last week, a butterfly danced my way!"

The daisies declare, with full belly laughs,
"Let's throw a party with the giraffe's half!"
They marvel at stars that twinkle so fine,
Releasing their secrets over sweet wine.

Each breeze carries chuckles, a soft serenade,
While crickets compose in striped masquerade.
"Listen closely," they say, "the trees love to share,
Those whispers of fun, a delightful affair!"

So wander through pathways of giggly greens,
Join the feast of laughter, with light-hearted scenes.
In Nature's embrace, let worries unfurl,
In this garden of whispers, joy's in a whirl!

## The Mystique of the Underbrush

In shadows deep, they start to sneak,
With spiraled leaves, a whispered peek.
Like tiny hats for woodland gnomes,
  They giggle softly in their homes.

A dance of greens, a playful tune,
They wear the mist, like a fluffy balloon.
With frolicsome steps beneath the trees,
  They swap their secrets with the breeze.

## Swaying Beauty in the Gloom


Beneath the boughs, they twist and twine,
In waggish ways, they cross the line.
With a flap and flap, they flutter wide,
Wishing for birds, to hop and glide.

When sunlight drips through leaves above,
They wiggle and giggle, a leafy love.
Their shadows dance in a playful spree,
Telling tales of woodland glee.

## Enchanted Greenery's Song

Upon the earth where fairies roam,
They nod and bow, a leafy dome.
With fingers outstretched, they wave hello,
To curious critters that come and go.

In this merry glade, laughter bubbles,
As critters tumble, escaping troubles.
With idle chatter, they sway in line,
Each leaf a joke, oh how they shine!

## Ferns in a Whispering Breeze

Under the sun, they twist and sway,
A dance of merriment, come what may.
In playful whispers, secrets shared,
A rustle of laughter, no one spared.

With every gust, they shush and sway,
Making the world a bright buffet.
They huddle close, in giggling clumps,
Each secret sprout, with joyful jumps.

## **Undulating Leaves of Lore**

In the garden, whispers grow,
Leaves tell tales, as breezes blow.
A dandelion with a grin,
Winks and says, "Let's spin, spin, spin!"

Each leaf a story, green and bright,
Chasing clouds, both day and night.
Ferns dance lightly, oh what a sight,
In their world, all feels just right.

## Swaying Silhouettes

Underneath the starry skies,
Swaying ferns put on disguise.
They're ninjas in the moon's soft glow,
Feeling stealthy, just for show!

With laughter in the evening air,
They do the cha-cha without a care.
Each frond a partner, oh so spry,
Who knew plants could reach so high?

## The Poetry of Growth

In soil beds where dreams can sprout,
Ferns are poets, there's no doubt.
With every inch of twist and bend,
They write haikus which never end!

Roots dig deep, they giggle and cheer,
Saying, "Look at us, we persevere!"
Their whispers float on gentle thrills,
As they sip up all the spills.

## **Peering Through the Petioles**

Peering from beneath the leaves,
A tiny gnome who never grieves.
He plays hide and seek with snails,
Whispering secrets in hallowed trails.

Through petioles, he waves hello,
While grasshoppers put on a show.
With giggles loud, they bounce and play,
In the grand ballet of a sunny day.

## Currents of the Canopy

Up above, the leaves do sway,
Squirrels dance in a playful ballet.
Branches creak like an old man's joke,
While shadows skip and giggle, bespoke.

The sunlight winks, then hides away,
A chameleon's stunt, gone astray.
Pigeons cluck like they've lost their way,
Should have taken a map, or a GPS, hey!

## Unfurling Dreams

In the garden, wishes sprout,
A snail's race makes all scream and shout.
With every twist, a secret as big,
A butterfly's dance, doing a jig.

The daisies gossip about the sun,
While worms wiggle, just having fun.
In this realm, the odd is the norm,
Laughing leaves in a joyous swarm.

## **Ferny Footprints**

Little critters leave their trace,
A beetle's ball with a bit of grace.
Tadpoles chuckle, a slippery show,
While mice in hats begin to stow.

Each footprint tells a tale absurd,
Of nightly feasts and flying birds.
In the thicket, jests take flight,
Even shadows can laugh at night.

## Rhythm of the Roots


Beneath the soil, the gossips thrive,
Moles compare who's taken a dive.
Roots hold hands in a tangled spree,
Tickling worms with glee, that's the key!

A crickets' band plays rustic tunes,
While frogs leap like silly cartoons.
All join in for a grand ballet,
Swirling 'round in earthy play.

## Chronicles of the Forest Spirits

In the woods, where whispers play,
Tiny sprites dance day by day.
They trip on roots, oh, what a sight!
Chasing shadows, giggles ignite.

With acorn hats and leaf-wrapped shoes,
They shout and cheer, they never lose.
A squirrel steals their lunch with glee,
Spirits pout, but then they flee.

Nestled deep in mossy beds,
They dream of cheese on merry spreads.
One spirit sneezes—oh, what a blast!
Shakes the trees, the fun's unsurpassed.

In moonlit nights, they prank the deer,
With silly songs that all can hear.
The forest echoes with laughter bright,
Chronicles of joy, a pure delight.

## Under the Umbrella of Green

Beneath the leaves, a world so bright,
Where critters giggle, what a sight.
A frog in boots jumps with flair,
He croaks a tune without a care.

A snail slow-dances, takes his time,
While ants march by, each in a line.
They stop to gossip on a twig,
'The caterpillar's now a wig!'

In puddles form, reflections play,
A pizza party, hip-hip-hooray!
But wait, the pies are all a bluff,
Made of moss and leaves—oh, that's tough!

Under the branches, tales unfold,
Of clumsy creatures, brave and bold.
With laughter shared, let joy convene,
In the shade of our umbrella green.

## Hidden Harmonies of the Woodland

In a thicket, soft songs sprout,
A raccoon sings, there's no doubt.
He strums a twig, it's quite a show,
While rabbits dance, their faces aglow.

A chipmunk claims the title of king,
Wearing a crown made of string.
He holds a court with silly jest,
And laughs about who snitched his nest.

Trees hum tunes of ages past,
But squirrels chatter, having a blast.
They drop acorns, and giggles ring,
Nature's band, what joy they bring!

Hidden voices blend and cheep,
Under the ferns, they all leap.
A woodland choir, hilarious and grand,
In perfect harmony, a playful band.

## Sheltering Shades and Serene Spaces

Under the boughs, where shadows play,
Turtles nap, dreaming all day.
A butterfly flits, can't find her friend,
She jokes, 'I think he's in a bend!'

The drumming of woodpecker's beat,
Rhythm of fun in the summer heat.
A hedgehog rolls, quite out of breath,
'Is this a game or near my death?'

The mushrooms giggle in a group,
Spreading laughter like a loop.
While a beetle moonwalks on a log,
Telling tales of the night like a frog.

In these shades of jolly embrace,
Life's a party, a joyous chase.
With shades so cool and smiles so wide,
Serene spaces where laughter won't hide.

## Flourish in the Forest

In the woods where squirrels play,
Leaves dance like it's a cabaret,
Roots twist and twine, they have their flair,
Trees gossip wildly, do they care?

Bugs wear tiny hats and ties,
Frogs croak jokes, oh what a surprise,
Mushrooms giggle, click their heels,
Nature's laughter is what appeals.

Rabbits bounce in a silly race,
Chasing shadows, quickening pace,
Breeze tickles, makes the branches sway,
In this wild party, who needs ballet?

So come join the woodland scene,
Where all things funny are evergreen,
With silly hats and loads of cheer,
Flourish here, you'll lose all fear!

## Spirals of Serenity

Twisting vines in a dizzy spree,
Whirling leaves sing in harmony,
Clouds drift by, quite carefree,
Mossy rocks join the jamboree!

Snails in shells with blingy charms,
Wobble forward, causing alarms,
Ladybugs with polka dot pride,
In this spiral, they cannot hide!

Dancing shadows, a wiggly sight,
Laughter echoes, day turns to night,
Nature's spirits spin and twirl,
Where serenity gets a giggly whirl!

Join the fun, take a twirl and sway,
In spirals where laughter won't stray,
With every giggle, you'll surely see,
Life's a dance, wild and free!

## **The Art of Being Green**

Not just the color, it's an art,
Leaves paint smiles, that's just the part,
Cabbage hats on broccoli heads,
In veggie land, there's laughter spread.

Lettuce lounges with style and grace,
Carrots do cartwheels, it's quite the race,
Spinach flexes, showing its might,
Even peas giggle, what a delight!

In gardens where the wacky grow,
Whether sun or rain, they steal the show,
Green thumbs wave, with joy they glean,
In this art, there's no in-between!

So come pick laughter from the vine,
With every bite, it's tasty and fine,
In this garden of glee, let's convene,
For the secret's out: be silly and green!

## Whispered Tales of the Thicket

In the thicket, secrets flutter,
Rabbits whisper, oh what a clutter,
Squirrels hide nuts, sharing their lore,
Tricky tales that make you roar!

Berries giggle, tickling tongues,
As owls blink and chirpy songs,
The wind howls jokes from tree to tree,
Nature's humor in harmony!

Grumpy hedgehogs roll with flair,
While chatterbugs swing in mid-air,
Ants march to the beat of fun,
In this thicket, laughter weighs a ton!

So gather 'round, lend an ear,
To whispered tales that bring good cheer,
In this playful wild, let joy be thick,
For laughter's the trick, oh what a kick!

## Echoes of the Ancient Fern

In the forest deep, they whisper and sway,
Old ferns giggle at the light of the day.
With leaves like hands, they wave to the breeze,
Hiding secrets, just like old trees.

A dance of shadows, they put on a show,
Tickling the toes of those who stroll slow.
"What's that smell?" a curious deer asked,
"Just the ferns laughing; they're truly unmasked!"

Their age defies time, they know all the tricks,
Telling tales of the past with their leafy antics.
Each rustle a giggle, each frond a great joke,
In the land of the ferns, laughter's no hoax.

So when you wander where the wild ferns grow,
Remember their humor, let your cares go.
Embrace the green giggles, the joy they impart,
Dance with the ferns, let them lighten your heart.

## The Dance of the Shaded Dream

Underneath branches, where shadows connect,
Ferns throw a party, with fun to expect.
They shimmy and twist in the cool evening air,
Wearing their green dresses without a care.

Under the moonlight, they giggle and prance,
Inviting the critters to join in the dance.
A rabbit hops over, thinks he's quite slick,
But ferns just chuckle, doing the old wiggle trick.

A caterpillar spins, what a sight to behold,
Flashing his colors, so brazen, so bold.
They all sway together, in perfect harmony,
Nature's own chorus, a giggling symphony!

The frogs croak along with each beat of the night,
The stars join the fun, twinkling so bright.
So if you find ferns in a shady old dream,
Join in the laughter, let your heart beam!

## **Verdant Dreams and Silent Streams**

Along babbling brooks, where the ferns like to play,
They gossip in whispers, oh what do they say?
"I saw a squirrel, he was quite the big cheese,
Dropping his acorns with effortless ease!"

In stillness they ponder, as frogs leap and croak,
Creating stories like a well-written joke.
Each frond has a secret to share with the air,
"Have you heard? Laughter's the best kind of care!"

While dragonflies giggle, fluttering high,
Ferns wiggle and nod as the clouds drift on by.
"Did you see the last leaf that danced with the wind?
He really did flail, seemed a bit unpinned!"

In the heart of the forest, where silence may gleam,
The ferns keep on dreaming, or so it would seem.
So stop by the stream, let your worries all fade,
Laugh with the ferns, in their leafy parade.

## Chlorophyll Chronicles


These chronicles whisper of tales gone awry,
Of ferns that once tried to learn how to fly.
They flapped their green arms, oh what a display,
But gravity laughed, and they landed in hay!

In the depths of the woods, they throw a fine feast,
Inviting the wonders, from great to the least.
"Come dine with us, mushrooms, and lichens fair,
We'll laugh until sunlight slips under the air!"

Each leaf tells a story, a laugh or a tease,
Of summers spent basking in warm, gentle breeze.
They gather together beneath the grand trees,
Creating a ruckus with whirls and with wheezes.

So if you feel heavy, or burdened and worn,
Just seek out the ferns, in the light of the dawn.
Embrace all their laughter, let each chuckle flow,
For in the world of ferns, there's a constant hello!

## A Tapestry of Fronded Fantasies

In a jungle of greens so fleet,
Frogs leap on their tiny feet.
Laughter echoes, bubbles fly,
As worms dance in a silly tie.

A leaf sneezes, what a sight!
It tickles bugs, oh what a fright!
Squirrels chuckle, chipmunks cheer,
In this patch, joy's always near.

The sun peeks through with a wink,
All the plants begin to think.
'What game shall we play today?'
Nature giggles in her play.

A tapestry spun with leafy cheer,
Among the roots, we dance in sheer.
Every frond has a tale to tell,
In this world, we laugh so well.

## Nature's Lush Embrace

Trees wear smiles in shades of green,
Their branches sway, a joyful scene.
A grasshopper sings a silly tune,
While petals prance beneath the moon.

Breezes tickle the tiny bees,
Who buzz and tickle through the trees.
The daisies wear crowns of misty dew,
As they dance in twirls of joy anew.

A snail races, but it's never fast,
He's got a shell; his role is cast.
With nature's laughter swirling 'round,
The earth giggles at what is found.

In this embrace, all creatures cheer,
Finding fun in the atmosphere.
Underneath the sun's warm grace,
Joy's found in every leafy space.

## The Poetry of Canopied Light

Sunbeams splash like playful cats,
Chasing shadows, high-flying bats.
Leaves whisper jokes where squirrels play,
Creating giggles, come what may.

A fox with a flair learns the tango,
With mushrooms clapping, what a show!
While daisies don hats made of clay,
Every flower is here to stay.

Bubbles of laughter rise up high,
Where clouds drift lazily in the sky.
As laughter weaves through the canopy,
All of nature joins the jubilee.

In this light, all spirits soar,
With nature's giggles, we explore.
The poetry flows, a natural sight,
Under this vibrant canopied light.

## Musings at the Edge of the Forest

Beyond the trees where shadows play,
The creatures joke and sway all day.
A turtle giggles as he strolls,
While acorns tumble, that's their goals.

The wind tells tales of silly schemes,
While mushrooms sprout with childish dreams.
In this corner where laughter sways,
Every critter joins in the plays.

A raccoon masks up for the show,
With a wink and a grin, he steals the glow.
The forest hums a merry tune,
As moonbeams dance upon the dune.

At the edge where fun does blend,
Nature's laughter has no end.
Together we muse and delight,
In the forest, all feels just right.

## **Verdant Reveries in Dappled Sunlight**

In a coat of leaves, the trees all dance,
Their roots tickle toes, in the grass they prance.
Squirrels host parties, with acorns galore,
While birds play tag, making quite a roar.

Sunlight winks down, through a leafy shade,
Dancing with shadows that never quite fade.
The rabbits all gossip, with whiskers so spry,
They laugh at the clouds that forgot how to fly.

## The Lament of the Olden Grove.

Oh, the old oak complains, with creaks and a groan,
Says it's not as spry, since the moss has grown.
The vines tease its branches, such a tangled mess,
While ferns roll their eyes, in leafy distress.

"It used to be lively," the sapling will say,
"But now it just snoozes the whole live-long day."
The bugs all agree, in a bug-laden throng,
While the toads sit in chorus, croaking their song.

## Whispers of the Woodland

The woods hold secrets, or so they declare,
A squirrel once whispered, "There's treasure out there!"
But all that he found, much to his chagrin,
Was a nut with a crack, he now wears as a pin.

The owls have gossip, they hoot and they sway,
Pondering if foxes just fancied gourmet.
While hedgehogs ponder the price of a shoe,
As they strut through the thicket, a fashion debut.

## Lush Green Reverie

In jungles of green, where the wild things roam,
A parrot named Phil claims this tree as his home.
He squawks at the sun, "I'm just here for the show,
And snacks from the visitors, don't you know?"

The ferns giggle softly, swaying like jesters,
While the grass tries to keep up with all of their festers.
As petals burst forth, in colors so bright,
The buds hold a contest, for best dressed tonight.

## Beneath the Fern's Embrace

In shadows deep where ferns do dance,
I trip on roots at every chance.
Their leafy laughter fills the air,
I pause to fix my tangled hair.

A critter pokes from underneath,
It asks me for a minty sheath.
I chuckle soft and share my snack,
And wonder how I wound up back.

With every twist, the ferns conspire,
To send me on this leafy tire.
They wave their fronds with cheeky glee,
Am I the joke? Oh, let it be!

But in their shade, I find my peace,
A giggling world that won't cease.
Together we will spin and sway,
In ferns and fun, we'll laugh away.

## Fern Fragments of Time

A whisper floats through time's own door,
Leaves giggle as they touch the floor.
They tell of days when Dino's roamed,
What a strange time, how I've moaned!

These clippings hold a history,
With tales of ferns and mystery.
Each curl and twist a silly rhyme,
While I just trip in summer's prime!

A splash of green, bright as my shirt,
I swat at flies—oh, that one hurt!
The plants conspire, no end in sight,
For every step, a ferny fright!

In fragments, they still tease my soul,
A leafy prank that takes its toll.
Yet in this green, I find my grin,
In every giggle, I join in.

**Tresses of Twisted Time**

With tresses that twist like a wiggly worm,
Each fern reveals a laugh, a term.
"Look at me," they seem to say,
"When you're lost, just join the fray!"

They curl and coil, oh what a sight,
I stumble twice, then take flight.
With every twist, my worries fade,
In this ferns' game, I'm not afraid.

They tickle toes as I walk by,
In a giggling crowd, I really fly!
"The skies are blue, but green is best,"
They chant with joy; it's all a jest!

So now I dance beneath their sway,
Twisted times lead me to play.
In every frond, a joke well-timed,
Their charm is silly and well-rhymed.

## Botanical Ballad

Oh, in the glade, the greens do sing,
A ballad bright, a lively fling.
With ferns that sway in joyful cheer,
They mock my steps and disappear!

Each leaf a note, a gentle tease,
While I trip over roots with ease.
"Join us!" they croak with a fluttering grin,
"Your dance is funny, let's begin!"

The flora laughs at my fine stance,
As I tumble down—oh, what a dance!
A botanical joke, I play my role,
With laughter sprouting from every hole.

So here I roam, in nature's hall,
With ferns that giggle, "Come, take a fall!"
In this ballad of green, I find my place,
With every stumble, I embrace the grace.

## Whispers of the Leafy Veil

In the garden, secrets sway,
Tiny creatures dance and play.
Leaves chuckle in the gentle breeze,
Nature's humor, sure to please.

A caterpillar wears a hat,
Thinking it's a fancy brat.
But when it tries to take a stroll,
It trips and rolls, oh what a toll!

The raindrops laugh, a gentle sound,
As puddles form upon the ground.
The grass tickles the bumblebee,
As it giggles loudly, 'Look at me!'

In shadows deep, the ferns all grin,
While squirrels plot their next big win.
With playful leaps, they chase their tails,
In this world where joy prevails.

## Beneath the Canopy's Embrace

Underneath the leafy shield,
A raccoon's got a meal revealed.
He tries to munch but makes a mess,
With berry juice, he looks a stress.

A family of ants march in line,
Carrying crumbs, oh so divine!
But one gets lost, starts to complain,
'Wait for me, this is such a pain!'

The sun peeks through with a bright grin,
While branches sway, the fun begins.
Birds join in with a cheeky song,
And even the shadows dance along.

Under the boughs, tales are spun,
Of mischief, laughter, and silly fun.
In the green realm where weirdness thrives,
Nature giggles; it's how she survives.

## The Green Symphony Unfolds

The orchestra of leaves complies,
As wind conducts beneath the skies.
With rustling sounds, they start to play,
A concerto that just makes your day.

A chipmunk's on the drums, quite bold,
While daisies sing, their petals gold.
The ants provide a steady beat,
Adding rhythm, oh so sweet!

The dandelions twirl and prance,
In the soft breeze, they take a chance.
But when a gust joins in their spin,
They scatter seeds, oh where've they been?

As melodies rise to meet the blue,
Nature's humor shines right through.
In this symphony, we find delight,
A playful tune that feels just right.

# Lush Elegy in the Shade

In the cool shade where ferns do grow,
A wise old turtle moves so slow.
He mumbles tales of days gone past,
And makes us laugh—his jokes are vast!

Mushrooms giggle, all in a row,
Telling stories that seem to glow.
With spots and colors, they have charm,
But watch your step! They cause alarm.

A fox in boots prances by with glee,
Singing aloud, 'Just look at me!'
But slips on moss, oh what a sight,
Rolling over, he's lost the fight.

Under the canopy, joy remains,
Where mischief lingers like summer rains.
In this lush realm, laughter's our friend,
Not an end, but a twist to blend.

# Echoes of the Underbrush

In the shadows where critters play,
Frogs croak jokes at the end of day.
Leaves giggle as they sway along,
The underbrush hums a playful song.

A raccoon winks with a cheeky grin,
While squirrels tease and do a spin.
Nature's laughter fills the air,
With every rustle, fun everywhere!

The grasshoppers join in a dance,
Jumping high as if in a trance.
A party of critters, oh what a sight,
Under the moon, they party all night!

So listen close as night falls near,
The whispers of the woodland cheer.
Echoes of giggles, a woodland spree,
Join the fun—come dance with me!

## Ferns in a Gentle Breeze

Ferns wave hello with fronds so bright,
In the warm breeze, what a delight!
They shimmy and shake, putting on a show,
Who knew plants had such rhythms to flow?

Tickled by wind, they laugh and sway,
Playing hide and seek in a sunny ray.
A critter peeks from behind a leaf,
Could it be a squirrel or a little thief?

With each rustle, there's humor to find,
Ferns acting silly, oh so unrefined.
Each twist and twirl brings a smile wide,
In nature's dance, we're all allied.

So take a moment, let laughter grow,
Join the ferns in their cheeky show.
In a gentle breeze, the fun does rise,
Nature conspires to brighten our eyes!

## The Elegance of Elongation

Tall and slender, ferns stand so proud,
Stretching their leaves, they draw a crowd.
With every inch, they pose and preen,
In the garden stage, they reign like a queen!

"Look at me!" they seem to shout,
As ants below scurry about.
With laughter echoing through the air,
Ferns know how to grab their share.

Prancing in the sun, what a sight,
Waving their arms, ready to ignite.
A comedy show in shades of green,
Ferns lead the act, an elegant scene!

So let's applaud their fancy flair,
These leafy ladies, full of air.
In the garden's heart, they stretch and sway,
Making us chuckle, day after day!

## Embrace of the Earth

Cuddled close in a cozy clump,
Ferns embrace the earth with a cheerful thump.
Calling all critters to come and play,
Sharing giggles as they tumble and sway.

With roots deep down, they find their charm,
Surrounding soil, oh, so warm!
Their leafy laughter fills the ground,
In their green haven, joy abounds.

A squirrel finds shade, takes a quick nap,
While worms wiggle in an earthworm trap.
The vibrant ferns wave to say,
Come join the fun in this earthy ballet!

With every breeze, they dance in glee,
Nature's hug feels so free.
In the embrace of the earth's nice spin,
Ferns invite everyone to dive right in!

## Tangles of Time and Moss

In a forest so lush, time takes a spin,
Moss carpets the ground, where antics begin.
A squirrel in slippers, a turtle in shades,
Dance under the leaves, in whimsical glades.

Old trees tell stories, all bent out of shape,
With branches like hands, they mime and escape.
The shadows all giggle, the sunlight won't quit,
As critters play tag—oh, what a funny skit!

In corners of ferns, secrets overflow,
Of rabbits who gossip, and toads in a row.
A snail with a mustache claims he's the best,
While the ants roll their eyes, too busy to rest.

With laughter and whispers, the forest does bloom,
In tangles of time, mischief finds room.
So come take a stroll, let your worries release,
In this realm of oddities, find joy and peace.

## Secrets of the Forest Floor

Beneath the thick foliage, secrets do lay,
Where acorns hold meetings at the end of the day.
A chipmunk with charm leads a lively debate,
While a pestering beetle just can't get a date.

In shadows, a fungus wears wisdom's gray hat,
As he chuckles at squirrels who chat with the cat.
Woodpeckers conduct a delightful old tune,
While mushrooms are dancing, just under the moon.

Frogs play the banjo, bugs hum along,
While daisies roll dice—yes, they've got it wrong.
With laughter and nature's sweet, silly ways,
The forest floor whispers of humorous plays.

So tiptoe and giggle through leaf-laden paths,
Find joy in the quirks of funny little maths.
The secrets of nature forever will soar,
Where laughter abounds, life's never a bore.

## **Fronds of Mourning and Joy**

In gardens of green, where the ferns often bloom,
A cactus complains, says he's stuck in his gloom.
Yet laughter erupts from the petals so bright,
As daisies recount their adventures at night.

A frond dressed in black, said he's seen it all,
While a dandelion dreams of a grand curtain call.
The roses convene for a gossiping spree,
While lilies roll dice, wanting a cup of tea.

"Why so glum?" chirped a sprightly young shoot,
"Your tales can't be that bad, don't wear that sad suit!"
Yet joy mingles softly with hints of the past,
As petals find humor that ever will last.

So dance with the fronds, those peculiar friends,
In mourning and joy, where the laughter transcends.
For life in the garden's a curious play,
Let's embrace all the quirks that come our way!

## Nature's Curled Embrace

In curves and in coils, the green world unfolds,
With laughter of leaves, and funny old molds.
A caterpillar joined a conga parade,
While shadowy figures found shade in the glade.

A vine tried to juggle, but tangled instead,
As posies all giggled, and swayed in their bed.
The wind took a bow, and the sun stole a dance,
While crickets chirped rhymes, giving night a chance.

Oh, the humor of nature, so keen and so bright,
With ferns making faces, a comical sight.
As mushrooms in hats offer cups full of cheer,
And clouds prance about like a jolly old deer.

So bask in the wonder, let joy be your chase,
In nature's embrace, find a warm, silly space.
For in every small moment, the laughter is sown,
In the curls and the twists, you're never alone!

## Embracing the Shade

Under leaves that sway and dance,
 I found my chance to prance.
With sunlight playing peek-a-boo,
 I giggle as the shadows grew.

A leafed umbrella, green and wide,
 My picnic spot, where I can hide.
With ants as guests, we share a bite,
And laugh at squirrels in their flight.

The breezy jokes the branches tell,
 Make grassy pirates laugh as well.
  In this shade, I'm free to roam,
  I've truly found my leafy home.

So cheers to green, with roots so bold,
 In the shade, the tales unfold.
Let's dance with joy, let worries fade,
 In laughter's arms, I'm unafraid.

## Canopy Chronicles

High above, the branches chat,
About the squirrel with a jaunty hat.
They share tales of fallen acorns,
And the time they tangled in the thorns.

A clever crow with shiny prize,
Befriends a lizard with tiny eyes.
In this leafy world, nothing's shy,
Where birds gossip and leaves sigh.

The shadows plot a funny prank,
While muddy boots make laughter tank.
Oh, the capers that they scheme,
In a woodland wonder, like a dream!

The sun's a fellow, peeking through,
Joining antics of the green crew.
With every rustle, joy is found,
In the canopy, silliness abounds.

## Murmurs of the Marshlands

In a marsh where squishy sits,
The frogs play leap and endless skits.
With cattails swaying, they take turns,
To share the tales of mud and ferns.

The turtles chuckle, slow and wise,
As dragonflies buzz with tiny sighs.
A gator grins, with quite the smirk,
While the herons file the quirky work.

The chatter there is loud and clear,
As crickets play their raucous cheer.
What a party in the muck,
Where every splash does bring good luck!

So wade on in, let laughter spread,
With muddy feet, let fun be led.
In this marshland, silly schemes,
We float on giggles, chase our dreams.

## The Veiled Green

Beneath the cloak of leafy hues,
There lurks a world of silly snooze.
With vines that giggle, tangles tease,
A green unveiled brings joyful pleas.

The mossy carpet, soft and plush,
Invites bare toes to dance and rush.
While mushrooms giggle, sprout and sway,
In this secret space, we laugh and play.

A gnome peeks out from leafy shade,
His garden jokes, a must-have trade.
With secret whispers from the trees,
In this veiled green, we float with ease.

So let's embrace this wondrous maze,
And share a laugh in leafy ways.
In this green, where joy's the theme,
We chase the light; we live the dream.

## Floating in a Ferny Dream

In a land where ferns do dance,
They sway and twirl in wild romance.
I stumbled in, tripped on a leaf,
Giggled loudly, felt such relief.

A fox in a hat, sipping tea,
Said, "You're quite clumsy, can't you see?"
The ferns laughed softly, a chuckling spree,
As I joined their ranks, feeling so free.

Rabbits in bow ties joined the fun,
Playing hopscotch under the sun.
They pranced and leaped, so full of cheer,
With ferns cheering loudly, "Come join us here!"

A turtle with shades got in the groove,
Dancing slow, with a charming move.
As leaves clapped along to the beat,
I knew this dream was quite the treat.

## Harmonies of the Hush

In the hush of the evening glow,
Ferns whisper secrets, soft and low.
A raccoon strums on a tiny harp,
Singing songs with a playful larp.

Owls roll their eyes, ready to snooze,
While the ferns giggle, sharing their views.
A band of frogs jump in surprise,
Croaking tunes that tickle the skies.

With dandelion hats and chic attire,
They twirl and jive by a leafy fire.
The night air bustles with laughter's breeze,
As ferns wink at stars with playful ease.

The raccoon bows low, takes a deep breath,
"Let's celebrate life, its joy—not death!"
And with that, they all morphed into jest,
Creating harmonies that never rest.

## Vines and Verses

Vines twist tales like spaghetti strands,
   Whispers stretch in creations grand.
A squirrel taps rhythm with cheeky flair,
   Bounding in stories, without a care.

The slugs are poets, dripping with ink,
   Crafting verses that make you think.
A breeze carries laughter, sweet as a pie,
As vines weave around, oh my, oh my!

A hedgehog recites with enthusiasm bold,
While ferns take notes, their tales unfold.
   With toothy grins and quills a-shine,
   In this enchanted place, all is divine.

As darkness falls, the verses ignite,
With giggles and snickers, under moonlight.
Together they create, with joy to disperse,
Every moment's a treasure in vines and verses.

## The Unseen Garden

In a garden hidden, with secrets untold,
Ferns wear disguises, feeling quite bold.
Pickles in top hats salsa with flair,
While marigolds chuckle, twirling in air.

A garden gnome with a mischievous look,
Writes poetry down in his little book.
The daisies roll over, making a jest,
As they play poker—who's lucky? The best!

Mice in tuxedos perform for the crowd,
As lilies cheer on, oh they're so proud.
With shadows that dance and twirls that ensue,
The unseen garden bursts with its view.

A thistle announces a wacky fair,
Where each stubborn weed proudly declares,
"Join us, dear friends, in this joyous spree,
In the unseen garden, forever carefree!"

## Gentle Giants of the Glen

In the glen where giants sway,
Leaves dance in a humorous play.
Whispers of laughter ride the breeze,
Tickling the branches, teasing the trees.

Moss-covered knees, a sight so grand,
With hats made of twigs, they take a stand.
They waddle and wobble, oh what a sight,
In their leafy costumes, they party all night.

Each rustle a giggle, each shake a loud cheer,
What's that on the ground? A lost shoe, oh dear!
With smiles so wide, they play hide-and-seek,
These gentle giants, so silly and meek.

So if you wander through this verdant spree,
Join the fun with a cup of sweet tea.
Laughter erupts where the tall ones groove,
In the glen of delight, come and move!

## Shades of the Silent Grove

In the grove where shadows play,
Trees wear shades that steal the day.
With roots that trip and leaves that grin,
They chuckle and wobble, inviting a spin.

A squirrel with nutty plans, oh what a chap,
Dances around with a comical clap.
Under the wit of a wise old oak,
The puns fly high as laughter is woke.

A breeze blows by with a cheeky tease,
Whispering jokes through the swaying leaves.
A rabbit had tea with a snarky fern,
In a circle of giggles, they share and learn.

So step inside this joyous retreat,
Where shadows come alive and tap their feet.
In the silent grove's delightful embrace,
The phantoms of fun dance with grace.

# **Tapestry of Tranquility**

In the tapestry where calm is spun,
Every thread has a joke and a pun.
Knots of laughter, stitched with glee,
In a quiet corner, come have some tea.

Petals gossip in hues so bright,
They tickle each other in shimmering light.
Butterflies flutter, their wings in a spin,
A comical race, where the fun begins.

The hummingbird chirps with playful flair,
Twirling in circles without a care.
Every flower has a story to share,
With winks and nudges, they entertain air.

So weave yourself into this jolly thread,
Where peace and humor are joyfully spread.
In this fabric of laughter, find your place,
Join in the fun, let your worries erase!

## A Symphony of Shadows


In the shadows, a symphony plays,
With croaking frogs leading the ways.
The crickets compose with chirpy cheer,
In the moonlight, the music is clear.

Owls hoot sweetly, like a tune so odd,
While behind them a sneaky, squirrel-like squad.
Rustling leaves join in with a wink,
As the night takes a pause to think.

Each shadow a dancer, each flicker a joke,
Balancing laughter, with the spook of an oak.
A melody of mirth swells up from the ground,
In the glimmer of the night, silliness found.

So, come hear the whispers in the dark,
As shadows organize their cheeky park.
In this orchestral night, never alone,
Join the symphony where giggles are grown!

## Secrets of the Shaded Dell

In the dell where shadows play,
Secrets whisper, come what may.
Ferns with faces, sly and bright,
Giggle softly, take their flight.

Beneath a leaf, a tiny crew,
All dressed up in morning dew.
They plan a party, oh what fun,
With leafy hats, they run and run!

A snail brings snacks, a bit of slime,
The slugs arrive, it's party time!
Mushrooms dance like they own the show,
While rabbits hop and try to glow.

But wait! A squirrel with nuts in hand,
Joins in too, the nutty band.
In this dell, such joy there's found,
Who knew plants could make such sound?

## The Silent Symphony of Sprouts

In the garden, sprouts emerge,
With a silent, leafy urge.
They sway and bend with playful grace,
Watch their concert, what a space!

Cabbages twirl in waltz-like ways,
While carrots host grand ballet displays.
Radishes giggle, hugging tight,
As peas pirouette, full of delight.

A beet hums low, a bass so bold,
While sprouts on stage spin tales untold.
Broccoli conducts, green and small,
In this silent symphony, they have a ball.

But just as finale takes its cue,
A breeze comes by, and oh, who knew?
The concert ends with laughter loud,
As veggies twinkle, feeling proud!

## Journey through the Jungle of Green

In a jungle lush and wide,
Where every leaf is a joyful ride.
Laughter echoes through the trees,
As critters dance upon the breeze.

Funky ferns in multi shades,
Playing hide-and-seek in glades.
Lizards wear their fanciest ties,
While parrots joke and tell their lies.

Monkeys swing from branch to branch,
Flipping through the ferns, a chance.
To sight the snappy, clappy crew,
Who'll crack a nut and giggle too!

And if you listen, keen and near,
You'll hear the laughter, loud and clear.
A party's brewing in this scene,
In the jungle, oh so green!

## Moments in the Moss

In mossy beds where secrets lurk,
Tiny critters do their work.
With each squish beneath your toes,
Funny stories come and go.

Mossy mugs for mushroom tea,
Sipped by gnomes with glee, oh me!
They share a giggle, toss a jest,
In this mossy, cozy nest.

Slugs compete in slow-motion races,
Chestnut hats upon their faces.
While ladybugs clap, wings in a whirl,
In this moment, life's a twirl!

So take a pause, feel the groan,
Of the mossy earth, a funny tone.
Unravel tales from greenish fluff,
In this world, it's never tough!

## Nature's Verdant Veil

In the lush and leafy land,
Critters dance with a grand plan.
A squirrel juggles acorns bright,
While birds hold karaoke night.

The trees laugh with a rustling sound,
As grasshoppers leap all around.
A snail slips, takes an awkward bow,
While butterflies cheer, "Wow, what a show!"

Fungi wear hats that are quite absurd,
And mossy couches, oh how they stirred.
A raccoon reads a book aloud,
To a giggling, enchanted crowd.

The sun peeks through with rays of gold,
The stories of nature feel like old.
Whimsical moments in every little scene,
In this place where laughter reigns supreme.

## The Gossamer Garland

A spider spins a dazzling thread,
Creating jewels above our head.
A butterfly wraps up a tall tale,
As bees buzz in with witty detail.

The daisies wear a crown of dew,
While frogs croak songs, fresh and new.
A chubby chipmunk sings in rhyme,
In this charming realm of verdant mime.

Worms throw a party in the soil,
As beetles boast of their daily toil.
Each leaf whispers secrets, clever and sly,
The garden's a circus, oh me, oh my!

Laughter bubbles in the creek,
With giggling fish who love to sneak.
In the gossamer light, all colors blend,
A magical moment without an end.

## Mysterious Groves

In the shadows of the ancient trees,
A raccoon reads poetry with ease.
A fox dons glasses, quite a sight,
As owls clap wings in sheer delight.

Whispers float on the crisp cool air,
As sneaky mice dart here and there.
A toad croaks puns beneath the moon,
And fireflies sway to a gentle tune.

The shrubs gossip about passing bugs,
While vines entrap some wandering hugs.
Mossy carpets hold unseen jest,
A treasure awaits, what's next in this quest?

With laughter echoing in every nook,
The groves are alive, come take a look.
Mysterious charm in every bend,
Nature's own jokes that never end.

## Enchantment in Green

Where the willow weeps and the daisies grin,
The wonders of nature spin tales within.
A heron strikes a breakdancing pose,
While laughing lilies strike a silly nose.

The woodpecker hammers an old funky beat,
As snails crawl by with their slow little feet.
The trees hold secrets, young and old,
In the shade, their stories unfold.

An ant parade marches in a line,
Each tiny twirl perfectly aligned.
The cherries burst into fits of laughter,
While dandelions dance—chasing after.

In every leaf lies a giggle concealed,
Nature's humor is perfectly revealed.
With charm in abundance, breezy and clean,
Adventure awaits in this world of green.

www.ingramcontent.com/pod-product-compliance
Lightning Source LLC
Chambersburg PA
CBHW071828160426
43209CB00003B/232